Measure Me

Jill Bever and Sheilah Currie

Pat and Atul are going to measure their bodies.

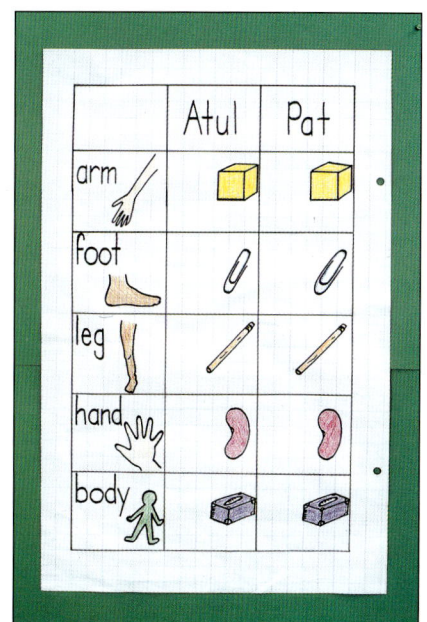

Here are the tools they are going to use.

Pat's arm is about 26 cubes long.

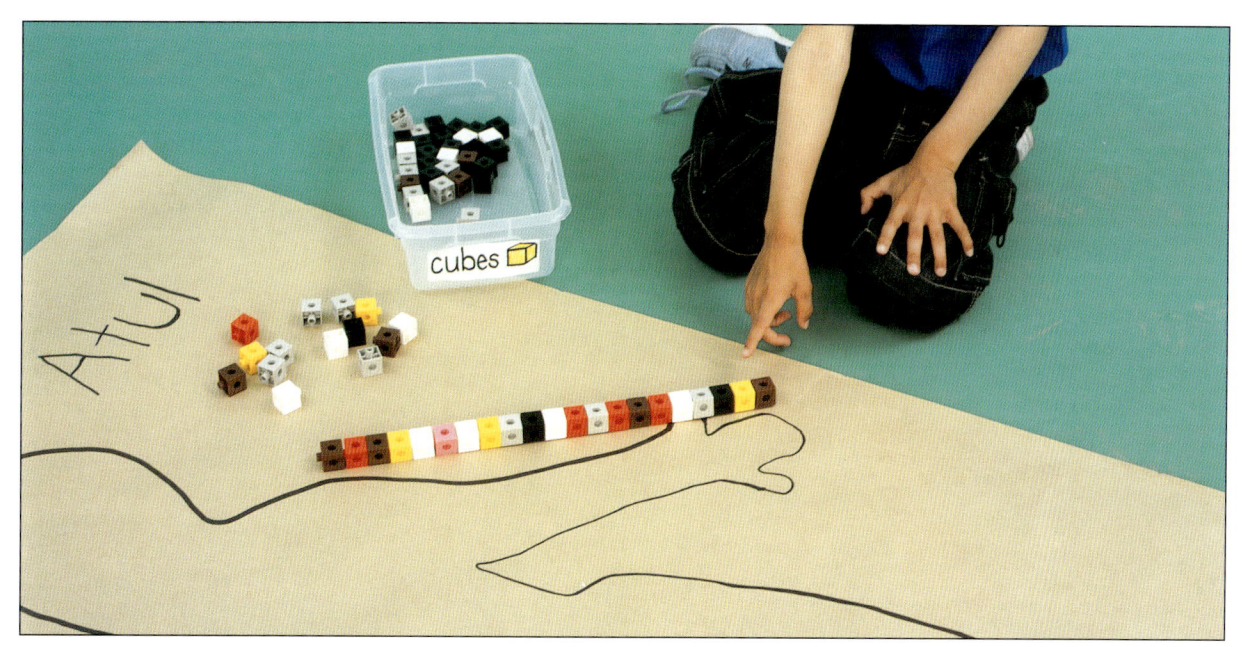

Atul's arm is about 21 cubes long.

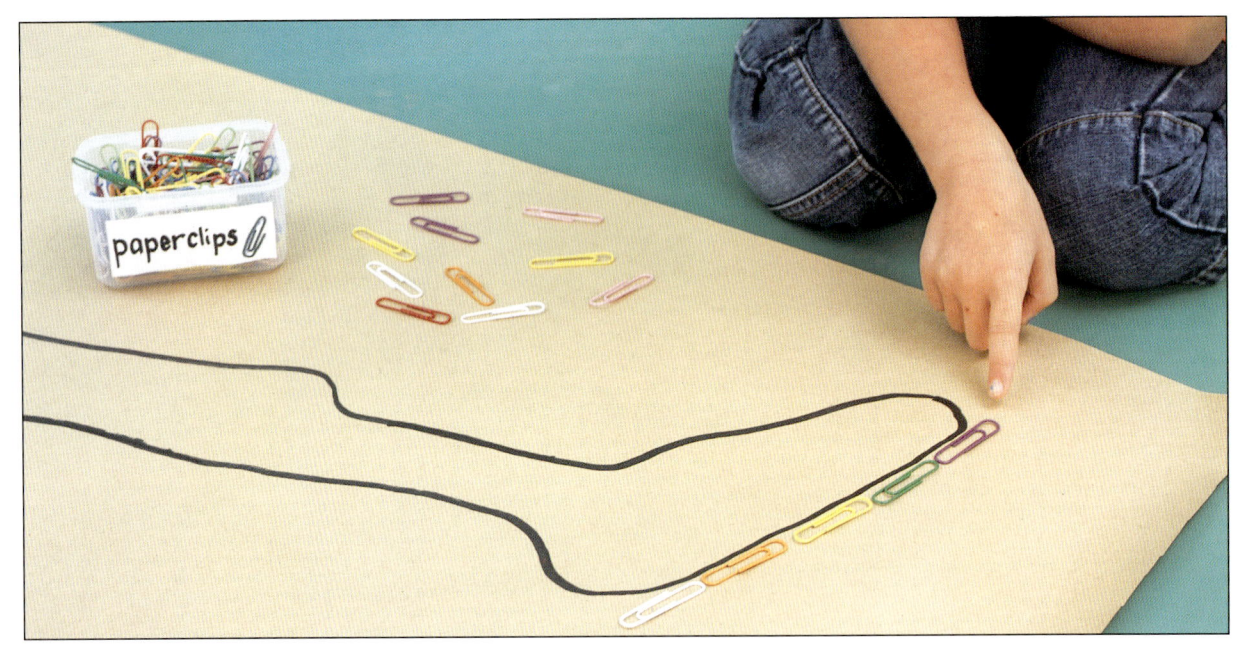

Look at Pat's foot.

It is about 5 paper clips long.

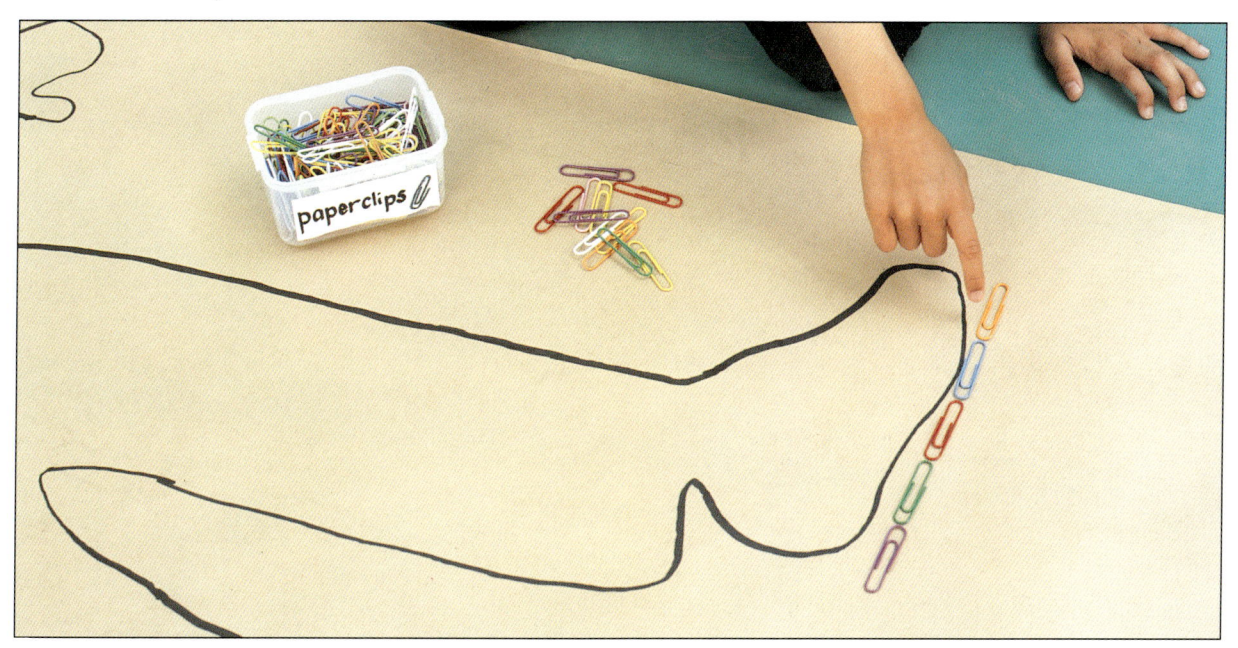

Look at Atul's foot.

It is about 5 paper clips long.

Pat's leg is about 3 pencils long.

Atul's leg is about 2 pencils long.

Look at Pat's hand.

It is about 9 beans long.

Look at Atul's hand.

It is about 7 beans long.

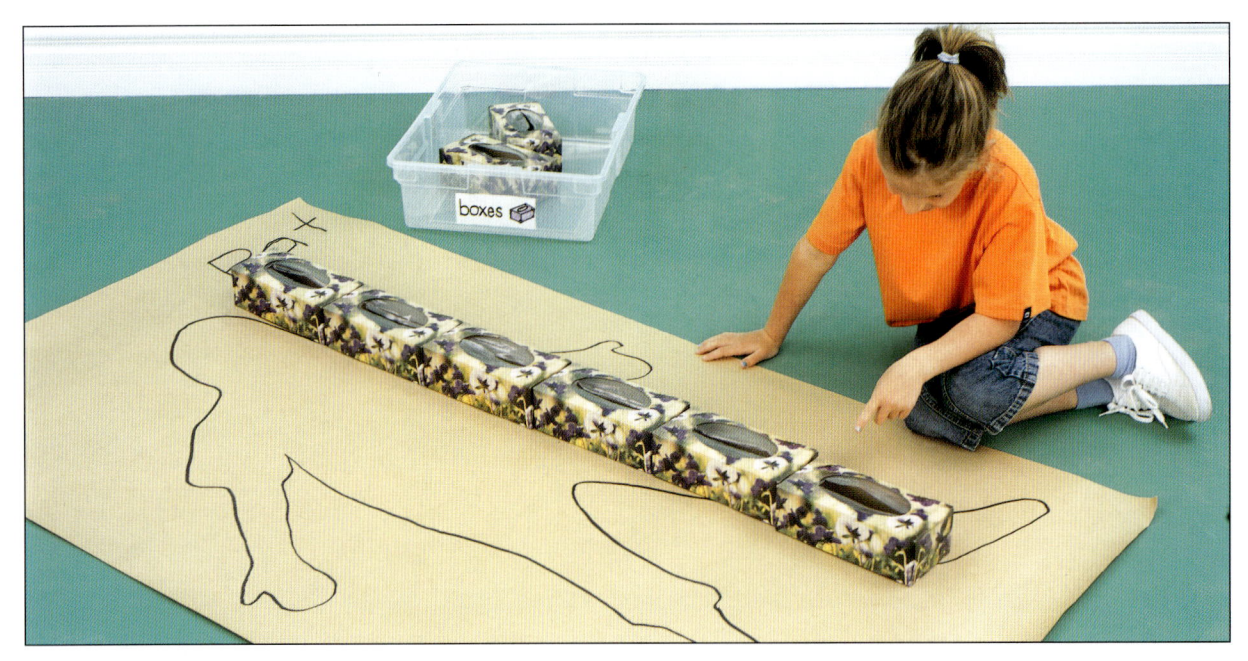

Pat's body is about 6 boxes long.

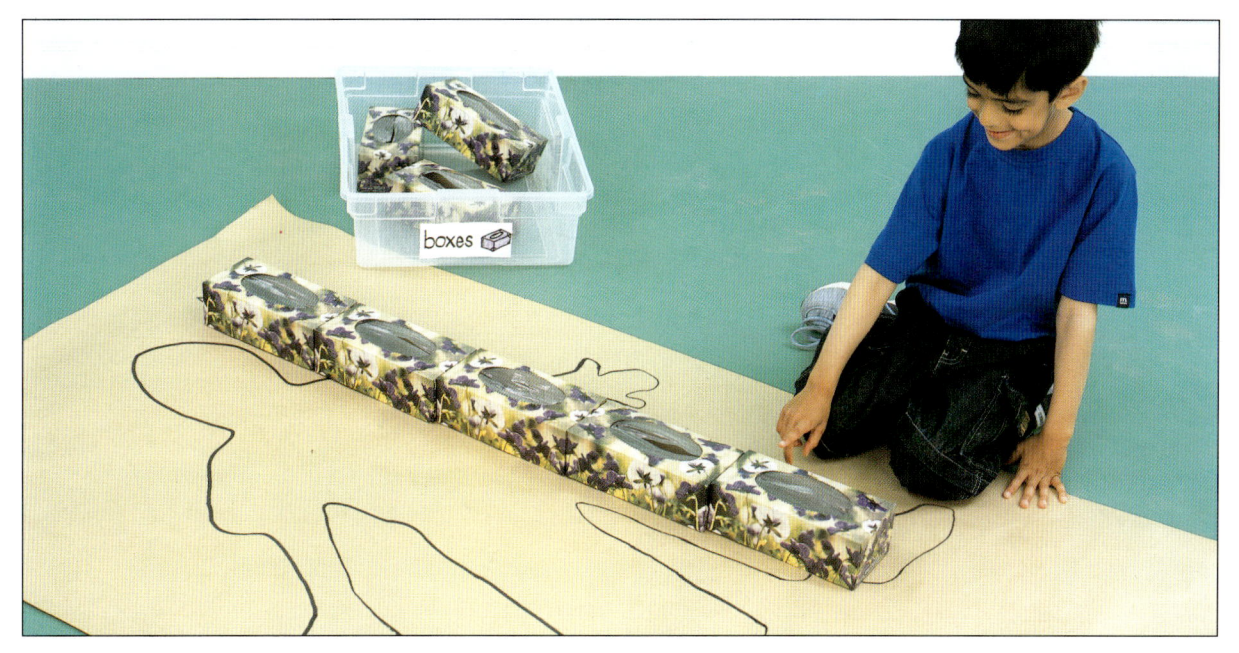

Atul's body is about 5 boxes long.

Atul is shorter than Pat.

Pat is taller than Atul.